MW00577565

COSTA RICAN
SPANISH
SPEAK LIKE A NATIVE!

¡PURA VIDA!
SE ME FUE LA PAJARITA
¡QUÉ CARGA! ¡TOME PA'L PINTO!
¡QUÉ CHIVA! ¿Al chile?
¡Qué dicha!
¡DEAY!
Se murió la flor. ¡Suave un toque! Con toda la
Ya me cayó la peseta. Cerrado como bombillo
Tengo un perro amarrado

LEE JAMISON

Visit us at www.insiderspanish.com

To the Jaén family,
for your love and friendship
and for having shared with us
all the delights of Costa Rican Spanish.

insiderspanish

Costa Rican Spanish

INTRODUCTION

TWO MEXICAN women were visiting Costa Rica for the first time. Referring to her daughters, the hostess at a family meal casually told them: **"No hagan caso de las güilas."** That answer—a vulgarity back in Mexico—made their ears stand on end. What they heard was: "Don't pay any attention to the *prostitutes*." But the real message was: Don't mind my *girls*. **Güila** is a generic term for a child, either a boy or a girl.

In another conversation hospitable locals told the Mexicans: **"¡Qué pecado! Vienen de muy lejos."** This literally means: "What a sin! You have come from so far." But for Costa Ricans, there is no sin in **pecado.** Here it means: *What a shame!* or *What a pity!*

The real shame is not realizing that in the global community generic Spanish is not good enough. Learning the country-specific peculiarities of the language is the

5

only way to avoid costly misunderstandings. The goal of the *Insider Spanish* series of books is to help you to do just that. Imitating regional speech dignifies the locals. And even though to them you are the foreigner, some may well come to regard you as one of the family. Your efforts will definitely be rewarded—many times over!

Are you thinking of visiting Costa Rica or are you living there now? Do you have family there or from there? Or are you just a language buff? Whatever the case, we urge you: Join the linguistic party! Instead of stubbornly clinging to phrase book Spanish, have an open mind! Embrace those new, but yet unfamiliar words and phrases! The more local words, phrases, and sayings you begin to use in your everyday vocabulary, the more you will fit in.

One size does not fit all

The avalanche of books on Spanish has left us knee-deep in a language that no one actually speaks. Real Hispanics don't read out of phrase books. To them they are stale bread. Everyday speech is full of color that is country-specific. Consider:

The generic word for "white" is **blanco.** But when describing a light-skinned person, Mexicans will instinctively use the term **güero.** In El Salvador, Nicaragua and Honduras they say **chele.** Panamanians say **fulo.** But in Costa Rica it's **macho** (though limited to blondes).

6

That's where the *Insider Spanish* series comes in. In this volume, we don't teach you Spanish; we teach you to make your Spanish *more Costa Rican*, to speak like a native. How? We have made an effort to identify 200 words and phrases that are endemic to the country. We cannot dogmatically state that they are only used in Costa Rica. Immigration agents don't detain words at the border, as if they had need of passports. Nevertheless, *as a group* they are like a fingerprint that unequivocally identifies the Spanish of any given country. For any Costa Rican who finds himself far from home, these words will be as captivating as the ringing bells of the ice cream salesmen.

Why 200?

One common saying is: **El que mucho abarca, poco aprieta.** It literally means: *He who tries to encompass a lot, squeezes a little.* The idea is that we shouldn't spread ourselves too thin. We give you 200 words and phrases because we want to satisfy your thirst—not drown you!

There is another consideration as well. My mother tongue is English and I have read many books on English words and sayings. And you know what? A large portion I have never heard in my lifetime! Never! Some Spanish language phrase books are just as all-inclusive. But how do you know if that phrase was known and used by 100 people or a 100,000? We save you the time by sorting that out for you. We hand you an eclectic selection to practice and perfect.

How to use this book

Costa Rican Spanish: Speak like a Native! is divided into seven sections. Check out the table of contents and jump to the one that most interests you. Others read just one entry a day and then try to practice that new word or phrase as soon as possible. That way you *own* it.

Only one or two terms appear on each page. This will help your focus. For many entries a literal meaning is provided. This often sounds unnatural in English, but can be an aid to memory. Sometimes we throw in a tip or two as to when using that phrase would be appropriate. Just a few pronunciations are provided for words that may initially throw foreigners for a loop.

In the main text, Costa Rican words and phrases appear in **bold type.** Shortly thereafter the translation of the phrase will appear in *italics*. In many cases, sample sentences were ripped right from the headlines or newspaper articles that have appeared in the Costa Rican press. *Insider Spanish* merely collects these quotes and they do not represent the opinion of the author. Since Spanish and English differ in punctuation styles, we here favor the English style even in Spanish quotes.

Lastly, feel free to use the terms listed here in everyday speech. Our selection is informal, but devoid of vulgarities.

Having understood this, dive in and enjoy!

ins*derspanish*

Costa Rican Spanish

TABLE OF CONTENTS

1

A CONVERSATION PIECE

¡Diay!

Pronounced dee-EYE

Ticos, the nickname Costa Ricans give themselves, seem to use this multipurpose term in nearly every sentence. At times, it is a call of protest, and in other contexts, it is a mere filler. **"¡Diay!** ¿Por qué no me llamó usted?"

Translation: *"Hey,* why didn't you call me?"

Person A: "¿Cómo está usted?"

Person B: **"Diay.** Más o menos."

Translation: A: "How are you?"

B: *"Well,* just so so."

¡Upe!

When you approach someone's home, what might you call out? Perhaps: "Hey, is anybody home?" In Costa Rica, just start shouting: **¡Upe! ¡Upe!**

abrirse

LITERAL MEANING: to open up

Here this verb takes on the additional meaning of *leaving*. It is a bit blunt, so use with caution. "Si no le gusta mi oferta, **ábrase.**"

Translation: "If you don't like my offer, you *can leave.*"

--- **RELATED TERMS** ---

jalar

Jalar also means *to leave*. That's the basis for this joke: How do you say mother-in-law in Arabic? The local answer is: "Ojalá **jalara.**" Translation: "I hope she *leaves.*" **Jalar** is also the verb for *dating*. If you keep that up, eventually you will have a mother-in-law!

andar a trole

Locals in jest call their foot a **trole.** So **andar a trole** means *to walk*. "Voy a **trole.**" "I am *walking.*" You could also say: **Voy trole-ando.** It means the same. Another option is **andar a pata,** which literally means to walk on your paws.

13

¡Qué pecado!

LITERAL MEANING: What a sin!

If someone were to tell you straight up: "What a sin!," you would likely feel judged. But not here, where it takes on the meaning: *What a pity!* or *What a shame!* The daily *La Teja* carried the following headline: "**¡Qué pecado!** Ballena se pierde y aparece en un río cerca de Londres." Translation: "*What a pity!* Whale is lost and then appears in a river near London."

furris

This is a local variation for **feo,** the word for *ugly.* It can also mean *dangerous.*

"¡Qué **furris** transitar por ese barrio!"

"It's *dangerous* to go through that neighborhood."

14

faja

In other Hispanic countries, you hold your pants up with a **cinturón** or a **cinto,** but not in Costa Rica. Here *belts* are known as **fajas.**

───── R E L A T E D   T E R M S ─────

cachos

Cachos literally means *horns* in Spanish. Locally, however, it's the term for *shoes.*

"¡Qué carga sus **cachos!**"

"Those are really cool *shoes!*"

Colgar los cachos means to hang up your shoes. If you do that, you are either *quitting a job* or *dying.* Yikes!

chema

In French, the word for shirt is *chemise.* The **ticos** borrowed and shortened it. A headline in *La Teja* announced: "En México sí saben de protocolo y le llevaron una **chema** con su nombre a la primera dama."

"In Mexico they know about protocol and they gave a personalized *shirt* to the first lady."

15

Calabaza, calabaza, cada quien para su casa.

LITERAL MEANING: Squash, squash, everyone back to his house.

Is that boring meeting finally over? If so, rattle off this childish rhyme. It's like saying: *Let's all go home!*

———— **RELATED TERMS** ————

¡Qué tigra!

LITERAL MEANING:
What a tigress!

What has been your experience visiting tigers at the zoo? See any vicious displays of ferocity? Most likely not. They are usually sleeping. With good reason, then, this animal exclamation means: *How boring!*

de patada larga

In the high-paced game of soccer, short passes are the norm. But when someone gets the bright idea of a long kick, that is, a **patada larga,** the ball seems to travel in slow motion. "La visita de mi suegra fue **de patada larga.**" "It seemed that my mother-in-law's visit *would never end.*" How pathetic!

Chepe

LITERAL MEANING: Joey

Men named José are often nicknamed Chepe. And the capital, San José, is not exempt from this treatment.

"¿Me hace raid hasta **Chepe?**"

Translation: "Could you give me a ride to *San José?*"

───── **R E L A T E D T E R M S** ─────

morado

LITERAL MEANING:
purple

The only thing you have to know about the color purple here is that it represents the Saprissa soccer team. The opposition will ask: "¿Está tuanis o **morado?**" Translation: "Are you OK or are you *a Saprissa fan?*"   Loaded question!

Chepito(a)

Don't confuse this with the capital's nickname. If you are called a **Chepito** or **Chepita,** it means you are a *busybody* or a *buttinsky.* "Hubo un accidente en la carretera y había un montón de **Chepitos.**" Translation: "There was an accident on the highway and there were a bunch of *rubberneckers.*"

17

chunche

If you forget every word in this book, remember this one! **Chunche** is the catch-all word for a *thingamajig* or a *whatchamacallit*.

"Páseme ese **chunche**."

"Pass me that *whatchamacallit*."

For extra credit, purse your lips together and use them to point to the item. They will think you are a local!

vara

Vara is another all-encompassing word. "¿Qué es la **vara?**" means: "What's the *deal?*" If you were to say this to someone on the street, it could provoke a fight.

Ask someone why he broke up with his girlfriend, and he might respond: "Es pura **vara**." Translation: "She's all *lies*."

19

¡La sacó del estadio!

LITERAL MEANING:
He kicked it out of the stadium!

In baseball, if you hit it out of the stadium, you're a hero! But if you kick the ball out of the stadium in soccer, you're an idiot! The objective is to score goals, not lose the ball. This clever metaphor means that one's answers are out in left field. "Cuando la profe preguntó a Ramón qué era la fotosíntesis, él dijo que no sabía nada de la fotografía. **¡La sacó del estadio!**"

Translation: "When the teacher asked Ramón what photosynthesis was, he said he didn't know anything about photography. *His mind was out to lunch!*"

Ya me cayó la peseta.

LITERAL MEANING: The quarter fell.

Back in the day before cell phones, we actually used coins to make calls from public telephones. In Costa Rica the price of a call was 25 cents, known here as a **peseta.** When that **peseta** fell, you got a dial tone. In many places jukeboxes worked on a similar premise.
Down to this day, **Me cayó la peseta** means:
It finally dawned on me. Another option is:
Me cayó el cuatro.

Se me fue la pajarita.

LITERAL MEANING:
The little birdie flew away.

Ever have an idea on the tip of your tongue and in an instant it vanishes? If so, you will have no problem understanding this idiom.
It completely slipped my mind.

Con mucho gusto

LITERAL MEANING: With much pleasure

In most Latin countries the typical response to **Gracias**
is **De nada.** But not here. **Ticos** will instinctively answer:
Con mucho gusto. Translation: *You're welcome.*
When thanking people, follow suit.

RELATED TERMS

chuzo

Chuzo means *beautiful* or *cool*
and is usually applied to
inanimate objects.

"¿Vio ese **chuzo** de
Mercedes Benz?"

"Did you see that
cool Mercedes?"

"¡Qué **chuzo** de casa!"

"What a *beautiful* house!"

corrongo

Corrongo is also *beautiful,* but
it can also be applied to people.

"¡Qué **corrongo** ese bebé!"

"What a *cute* baby!"

"Me encanta el cachorrito que
te regalaron. Es tan **corrongo.**"

"I love that puppy that they
gave us. It is so *cute.*"

Liga

LITERAL MEANING: League

In 1821 when word came that Mexico was liberating itself from Spain, a controversy was born. Should Costa Rica join Mexico or would it be better off as an independent republic? At that time both San José and Alajuela were part of the **Liga Republicana,** or Republican League. Since Alajuela native Gregorio José Ramírez gave the League its name, to this day Alajuela is known by its nickname, **la Liga.**

manudo

LITERAL MEANING: big-handed

Shortly after the **Guerra de la Liga,** which resolved the controversy mentioned above, people from Heredia started to claim that Alajuela residents had "la mano larga," literally, a long hand. The accusation? They had stolen property. To this day, **manudo** is the *nickname for Alajuela residents.*

mejenga

The national soccer team has qualified for the World Cup five times since 1990, thus creating a local soccer craze. As a result, the *informal soccer game,* known as a **mejenga,** is ubiquitous. Someone posted the following on social media: "Cualquier sitio sirve como cancha de fútbol. A los **mejengueros** nos da igual la playa, el potrero o la plaza del pueblo." Translation: "Anyplace can serve as a soccer field. For us *informal soccer players,* a beach, a cow pasture, or a public square is fair game."

RELATED TERMS

darle al mundo

What an exciting moment! You're in the midst of a soccer game, and the ball suddenly is at your feet. You prepare to strike that checkered sphere, sure to get a goal. But as you kick, you strike the ground instead. In local terms, **usted le dio al mundo.** *You choked!*

dar pelota

Nothing is more exhilarating than getting the ball. So when a local figuratively gives it to you, it means that he is paying attention to you, perhaps to the point of flirting. **"Déle pelota a** María. Está enamorada de ti." *"Pay attention* to María. She's in love with you."

hablar paja

LITERAL MEANING: to speak straw

How much does a piece of straw weigh? It probably wouldn't even move the scale! That's why Costa Ricans call both *harmless gossip* and *lies* **paja.**

"Las abuelitas pasaron toda la tarde **hablando paja.**"

"The grandmas spent all afternoon *shooting the breeze.*"

---------- **RELATED TERMS** ----------

batear

In baseball, hitters need the reflexes of a housefly. In a split second they must decide if they will swing or wait for the next pitch. When they do swing, they might get lucky and hit it just right. So when a local says: **Bateé la respuesta,** he means he *guessed the right answer.*

¿Al chile?

Chile, or *hot pepper,* is nothing to play around with; there is a certain seriousness associated with it. Hence, this is the common response to many questions. "Oyó que Yoli está encinta?" **"¿Al chile?"** "Did you hear Yoli is pregnant?" *"Really?"*

con toda la pata

LITERAL MEANING:
with the entire female duck

Rigoberto Guadamuz relates in *Diario Extra* that in the 1960s PRIM detergents came out with an advertisement in which a duck who had washed her clothes rested in a hammock. The piece ended with the lyrics: "PRIM está con toda la pata." Translation: "PRIM is with the entire duck." As a result, **con toda la pata** means *in great shape*. When someone asks how you are, just respond boldly: **¡Con toda la pata!** Don't worry; they won't think you're a quack. Sorry, if you had seen that one coming, you probably would have ducked.

¡Estoy puros dieces!

LITERAL MEANING: I am pure tens!

In Costa Rican schools students receive grades based on a one to ten scale, ten being the highest grade. So imagine the delight of a parent whose child had received straight tens! That's the idea behind this common response to **¿Cómo está?** It's akin to saying: *"I've never been better!"*

¡Ahí la tiene!

LITERAL MEANING: There you have it!

Picture this: A local gives you a sincere compliment on your shirt: "¡Está chiva esa chema!" That means: "That shirt is beautiful!" Just respond with: **¡Ahí la tiene!** It's the equivalent of saying *Thanks!*

Grammar tip: If the item is a feminine word in Spanish, use **la;** if it's masculine, use **lo.**

Está cayendo pelo de gato.

LITERAL MEANING:
Cat hair is falling.

When torrential rains come, in English we say that it is raining cats and dogs. But in this part of the world, cat hair falls. This weather metaphor
means: *It's drizzling.*

––––––––– **R E L A T E D T E R M S** –––––––––

garuba

Asdrúbal Quesada Castro wrote: "Una escasa **garuba** mojaba los herrumbrados techos de las casas del pueblo." Translation: "A fine *drizzle* moistened the rusty roofs of the town's homes."

Garuba, then, is a synonym for **pelo de gato.**

baldazo

A **balde** is a *bucket*, so a **baldazo** is a *bucketful.* The daily *La Teja* reported: "El huracán Irma nos tiene en un puro **baldazo.**" "Irma has brought us nothing but *torrential rains.*"

If rains are intense, just say:
"¡Qué baldazo!"
"What a downpour!"

Regáleme...

LITERAL MEANING: Give me as a gift...

Usually when a Hispanic says **Regáleme,** he is
requesting a freebie. After all, the noun form, **regalo,**
means *gift*. But not for the **ticos**. Here **Regáleme**
means: *Give me*. It is understood that you will pay for
the item. **"Regáleme** una birra."
Translation: "I'll *have* a beer."

RELATED TERMS

teja

A **teja** is literally a *roof tile*. But
here it means much more. It
is an informal term for the
100-colon coin. But it can refer
to *100 of anything*. In fact, since
100 represents completeness,
if someone asks you how your
trip was, just exclaim: **¡Fue
una teja!** *"It was great!"*

¡Qué atraco!

This literally means: *What a
robbery!* But you may find this
saying handy, since locals will
try to charge you, the foreigner,
outrageous prices. When the
offer is ridiculous, just say:
¡Qué atraco! It's the equivalent
of: *"What! Are you trying
to rob me?"*

No se haga el ruso.

LITERAL MEANING: Don't make like a Russian.

Poor Vladimir arrives and doesn't know a lick of Spanish. Talk to him all you want, and you will get zero results. It's no surprise, then, that this means *to ignore*.

"Estoy hablando con usted. **No se haga el ruso.**"

"I am talking to you. *Don't play dumb.*"

——— R E L A T E D   T E R M S ———

¡Guachin pupilas!

The first word of this idiom comes from the English *watching*, and **pupilas** are *pupils*. Together the phrase means: *Watch out! Be careful!*

A derivative of the phrase are **guachos,** a local word for the *eyes*. And a **guachimán** uses his eyes wisely: He's a *watchman!*

¡Póngase vivo!

This literally means: *Make yourself alive.* And if you indeed are alive, you will be well aware of what is happening around you.

"¡Diay! ¡**Póngase vivo!**"
Translation:
"Hey, keep your eyes peeled!"
So don't a deadbeat. Stay alert.

29

¡Zóquele!

LITERAL MEANING: Tighten it!

You're riding your motorbike on the highway and you realize you are late for an important meeting. It's time to step on it! What will you do with your grip on the handlebars? Definitely you will tighten up. That word picture should help you to remember that **¡Zóquele!** means: *Step on it!* or *Hurry up!*

---- **RELATED TERMS** ----

soplado

Your plane is late, but the pilot announces that due to a favorable tailwind, you should make it on time. Similarly, **soplado** literally means *blown*. The implication is that you are moving as if a tailwind were pushing you forward. **Soplado** means *super fast.*

tallado

Tallado primarily means *carved*. But when we dress in tight clothing, we give the impression we have been carved into place. That's how **tallado** came to mean *tight*. And here what is especially tight is one's time. **Voy tallado** means: *I'm really pressed for time.*

30

usted

LITERAL MEANING: You (formal)

It is no exaggeration to say that this pronoun is more used locally than in any other country. Why? Most Latins limit its use to speaking with strangers or to older persons, as a sign of respect. Here, however, it is used with everyone. Married couples use it to address one another. Even parents call their small children **usted,** something unheard of elsewhere. So play it safe and speak to everyone as **usted**—even to your dog!

---------- RELATED TERMS ----------

vos

While **usted** is used with everyone, **vos,** the *informal you,* transmits great familiarity among friends. It is more common up north, close to the Nicaraguan border. Only use it if others address you as **vos**.

mae

Pronounced like the English word *my,* **mae** means *dude.* At the Manuel Antonio National Park I noticed that all the guides called one another **mae.** But, due to its informal nature, use it with caution, if at all.

muerto

LITERAL MEANING: a dead man

You are driving on the highway and suddenly your
local co-pilot exclaims: **¡Cuidado! ¡Hay un muerto!**
This literally means: *Watch out! There's a dead man!*
You scan the highway, but no corpse in sight.
Relax! Here a **muerto** is the term for a
speed bump, which straddles the road like
a lifeless body and gets you to stop.

──────── **RELATED TERMS** ────────

de viaje

Though this is the standard
phrase for **traveling,** here it
means *completely* or *totally.*
"De viaje se nota que
es un zaguate."
"It's *obvious* that
it's a stray dog."

volar caite

A **caite** is a *primitive sandal,*
worn by the poor. But today,
volar caite, literally fly the sandal, means *to take a long walk.*
By the way, if something is far
way, **ticos** say **largo** instead of
the standard **lejos.**

2

ALL IN THE FAMILY

echar el cuento

How do you convince a girl that you love her? That has been the subject of songs and movies the world over. Locally, you achieve this goal by telling a good story, or **cuento.**
"Pedro fue a **echar el cuento** a María."

Translation: "Pedro went to try to
woo over María."

RELATED TERMS

apretarse

This verb literally means
to squeeze together. Here it
means *to make out.*
"Pedro terminó **apretándose**
con María."
"Pedro ended up *making out
with* María.

cabra

A **cabra** is a *female goat.* But
here it's a derogatory term
for *girlfriend.* If all goes well
for Pedro, María will become
his **cabra.** Pedro likewise will
become María's **cabro,**
or *boyfriend.*

cumiche

This comes from a Nahuatl word which means "little skirt." Centuries ago, before the advent of modern clothing, each child wore a skirt, and the baby of the family logically had the smallest skirt of all, and hence the term.

"Rachel es la **cumiche** de la familia."

Translation: "Rachel is the *baby* of the family."

RELATED TERMS

chineado

Chinear means *to hold in one's arms,* as is typically done with a baby. But if some parents continue to baby their child even when he leaves infancy, then the child is said to be **chineado,** or *spoiled.*

chingo

Don't be alarmed by this word, which locally is completely innocent; it means *naked.*

"No ande **chingo.**
¡Póngase ropa!"
"Don't walk around *naked.*
Put on some clothes!"

güila

Pronounced WEE-lah

This is the standard word for *boy* or *girl*.

"Dígale a esa **güila** que se venga."

Translation: "Tell that *girl* to come here."

Grammar tip: If referring to a boy, use **el** as the definite article, and **la** if it is a girl.

———— **RELATED TERMS** ————

guato

Pronounced WAH-toh. The local term for *dog.*
"Salió un vecino a pasear el **guato** y lo multaron."

"A neighbor went out to walk his *dog* and they fined him."

Doggonit!

macho

There's no chauvinism associated with **macho;** here it means *a blonde.*
"El bebé salió **macho** como su papá." "The baby turned out to be *blonde,* just like his father."

For women, use **macha.**

Se devolvieron los peluches.

LITERAL MEANING:
They returned the stuffed animals.

As part of the dating process, couples exchange gifts, possibly even a stuffed animal or two. But what if things don't work out? They just return the presents.

"Después de jalar por dos años, Pedro y María **se devolvieron los peluches.**"

Translation: "After dating for two years, Pedro and María *broke it off.*"

novio de llavero

LITERAL MEANING: key chain boyfriend

These days kids seem to be growing bigger and taller than other generations. And that can create some mismatches. If a girl is substantially taller than her boyfriend, then he is a **novio de llavero.**
He's a shrimp compared to her.

marcar

If you are a working stiff, you know the drill. Go to work, punch in, slave all day, and then punch out. Our lives are controlled one time card punch at a time. Some girlfriends and their parents are just as controlling.

"Pedro está **marcando** con María."

"Pedro is *spending time with his girlfriend* María."

pedir cacao

LITERAL MEANING: to ask for cocoa beans

When a couple breaks up, it is possible that one of the two wishes that the relationship would continue.

"Pedro se fue a **pedirle cacao** a María."

"Pedro went to María *to ask for a reconciliation.*"

Se jalaron una torta.

LITERAL MEANING: They pulled a cake.

In these parts **torta** also means a *big problem.*

"Pedro y María **se jalaron una torta.**"

Translation: "Pedro and María *got themselves into a big mess; she's pregnant.*"

Of course, it can refer to any major difficulty.

39

No hay tu tía.

LITERAL MEANING: Your aunt is not around.

Centuries ago the Spaniards brought with them an aloe
vera-based medicine called **atutía.** This sounds like
a tu tía, *to your aunt.* Since the medicine was a sort
of panacea, when no solution was available, people
would say there is no **atutía.** So if no solution is readily
apparent, just declare: **No hay tu tía.** It means:
We will just have to make do.

hijo de papi

This literally means a *daddy's
boy,* and means the same here
as in English. "Ese **hijo de papi**
no estudia ni trabaja. No hace
nada." "That *daddy's boy* doesn't
study or work. He does
nothing at all."

Se le juntó el ganado.

A ranch owner wants his cattle
spread out. If they all were to
gather in one spot, it would be
a problem. "A Elena **se le juntó
el ganado** en el súper." "Elena
ran into all her ex-boyfriends at
the supermarket." What a beef!

3

A HARD
DAY'S WORK

brete

Francisco Malespín was a Salvadorean military officer and politician who lived during the first half of the 19th century. Perhaps his greatest claim to fame was the invention of a secret code that was used to communicate with his men. In the code, certain key letters were changed: A for E, I with O, M with P, F with G, C with S, and T with B. In this code, **trabajo,** or *work,* would become **breteji,** or **brete** for short. So, **¡vamos al brete!** *Let's go to work!*

---------- **RELATED TERMS** ----------

camello

Pity the poor camel. This beast of burden toils endlessly, walking mile after mile through deserts as it carries heavy loads, patiently waiting for its next drink of water. Thus, here it is a *person who is a slave to his work.*

pegarse un morón

Literally, this means *to be bruised.* But here it has come to mean *an enormous effort.* "José **se pegó un morón** para terminar a tiempo."

"José really *killed himself* in order to finish on time."

42

estar de Bagaces a Liberia

LITERAL MEANING:
To be going from Bagaces to Liberia

The cities of Bagaces and Liberia are in the northern part of the country. But the important thing to know is that Bagaces sounds like **vago,** which means a *bum.*

If someone is **de Bagaces a Liberia,** it means he is *bumming around.*

RELATED TERMS
---

clavado

This literally means *nailed.* It is quite the opposite of going to Bagaces! In this case, you are nailed to your work. "No sé cuándo llegaré. Aquí estoy **clavado.**" "I don't know when I'll get there. I'm *stuck at work.*"

hecho leña

Need firewood? Just get your ax and chop away! Likely what you bring home will be a splintered mess. And that's how we feel when we are exhausted. "Estoy **hecho leña.**" "I'm totally *wiped out.*"

43

falta de cancha

LITERAL MEANING:
lack of field

Soccer is king in Costa Rica! And the more time you
are on the field, or **cancha,** the more experience you
acquire. "¡Uy, **me faltó cancha!**
No compré los boletos a tiempo."
Translation: "Dang, *I messed up.*
I didn't buy the tickets in time."

gastar pólvora en zopilotes

LITERAL MEANING:
to waste gunpowder on buzzards

Gunpowder and other ammunition aren't cheap. So if
you buy some, you better get a deer or something worth
eating. Who would fire at buzzards? That would be a
pathetic *waste of time.* That is the meaning behind
this colorful word picture.

choricear

LITERAL MEANING: to make sausage

The sausage maker grinds up pork and stuffs it into the sausage casing of his choice. But what if he gets a little greedy? Could he introduce a bit of ground meat of inferior quality? The temptation is always there. That's why **choricear** in Costa Rica means *to sell pirated goods.* And the one carrying out the dirty deed is called a **choricero.**

───── **RELATED TERMS** ─────

chinamo

An *informal workplace.* "¡Ya estoy cansado, así que por hoy se cierra el **chinamo.**" "I'm tired now, so for today I am closing the *stand.*" Can't beat self-employment, right?

a medio palo

This literally means *at half stick.* It refers to a job that is incomplete. "Juan estaba construyendo su casa, pero le quedó **a medio palo.**" "Juan started building his home, but it was *left unfinished.*"

45

maría

Back in the days before taxis, you would have to call and request a ride. Urban legend has it that in the 1950s a certain María Brenes received such calls in San José and would dispatch a driver. Later when taximeters became popular, it was natural to call them **marías,** in honor of Ms. Brenes. "El taxista me cobró menos de lo que marcaba la **maría.**"

Translation: "The taxi driver charged me less than what the *meter* indicated."

———— **RELATED TERMS** ————

llave maya

Sometimes brand names can morph into common nouns. When USB flash drives were first introduced in the country, the Taiwanese brand Maya was popular. To this day any *flash drive* is a **llave maya.**

lata

Today's vehicles are so light that we are traveling in mere cans. This is the local term for the *bus.* "Llegué tarde porque venía en una **lata** de bus." "I got there late because of the *old bus.*"

Le serrucharon el piso.

LITERAL MEANING:
They sawed the floor out under him.

In a dog-eat-dog world, some workmates will stop at nothing to get your job. In Costa Rican Spanish, you might have the floor sawed right out under you! "Pedro **le serrucha el piso** a cualquiera con tal de ascender."

Translation: "Pedro will *undermine anyone's position* to try to get ahead."

Le van a cortar el rabo.

LITERAL MEANING:
They are going to cut your tail off.

If animals could talk, likely none would be in agreement with having their tails cut off. That would be painful and embarrassing. For us humans losing our jobs is equally distressing. "Trabaje duro o **le van a cortar el rabo.**"
Translation: "Work hard or *they will fire you.*"

Mucho rinrin, y nada de helados.

LITERAL MEANING:
Ring, ring, but no ice cream.

As a child there's nothing more thrilling than hearing the ringing bell of the ice cream salesman who pushes his cart through your neighborhood. But what if when you get there, he's all out? What a disappointment! This clever saying means: *He's all bark, but no bite.* Yes, that person is nothing more than a *smoke blower.*

─────── **RELATED TERMS** ───────

¡Qué bañazo!

A car zooms by and splatters you with the contents of a nearby puddle. Embarrassed? Of course. That's the idea behind **bañazo.** "Elena cayó en la pasarela. **¡Qué bañazo!**" "Elena fell on the runway. *How embarrassing!*"

brocha

A **brocha** is a *brush.* Here when you want to butter someone up, you apply it with a figurative brush. "Katia es una **brocha** en la escuela. Con razón, saca buenas notas." "Katia is a *suck-up* in school. No wonder she gets good grades."

¡Suave un toque!

LITERAL MEANING: Soft a touch!

Locally a **toque** is a *moment*. So this common phrase just means: *Hold on a second!* Figuratively, it could also come across as *Take it easy!* or even *Chill out!*

¿Me da su chayotera?

LITERAL MEANING:
Would you give me your squash vine?

This is a humorous way of asking for someone's signature, many of which are more twisted and tangled than the local squash vines.

49

sudar la gota gorda

LITERAL MEANING:
to sweat the fat drop

In Costa Rica's tropical climate, it doesn't take much to break out a sweat. It is no wonder that this metaphor is all about hard work. "Para ganarse el sustento hay que **sudar la gota gorda.**"

Translation: "To make a living, you've got to *work hard.*"

RELATED TERMS

polaco

A **polaco** is literally a *Pole*, as in a native of Poland. Here, however, it refers to a *traveling salesman* who generally peddles clothing and other goods on credit and comes right to your doorstep.

Se murió la flor.

Who doesn't like receiving flowers? You put them in a vase, enjoy their presence and aroma, but eventually they die and we throw them out. That's why this metaphor means: *It's a done deal.*

insider*spanish*

Costa Rican Spanish

4

FOOD FOR THOUGHT

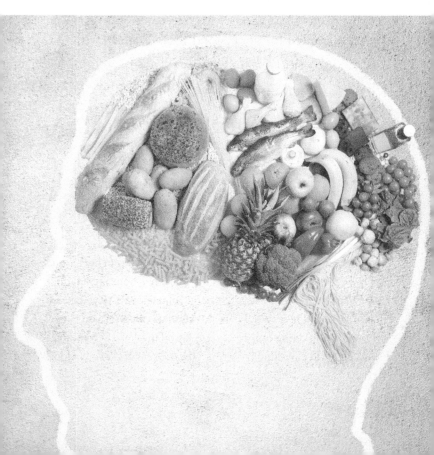

¿Cómo está el arroz con...?

LITERAL MEANING:
What's the rice like with...?

Here rice is served daily. But in a non-food context, this means something else. In an article in *La Teja* the writer's objective was to "entender **cómo está el arroz con** respecto a los piratas y los uberianos." Translation: He wanted to "understand *what's the deal* with the pirates and Uber drivers."

RELATED TERMS
---

casado

Casado literally means *married*. Here it refers to a *local dish of rice, beans, with either meat, chicken, or fish and garnished with salad*. But here's a question: If I stop eating **casado**, do I have to pay alimony?

chiverre

This is the term for *a local squash,* which roughly has the shape of a watermelon. But if someone says to you: **¡Qué clase de chiverre!,** you better lay off the squash! It means: *What an enormous belly!* Oops!

corcor

Here's an example of local onomatopoeia, that is,
a word that mimics the sound that it represents.
In this case, **corcor** is the sound of someone
chugging down his drink.

"Agarré un vaso de agua y me lo tomé **corcor.**"

Translation: "I grabbed a glass of water
and *chugged it down.*"

RELATED TERMS

birra

Technically the word for **beer**
is *cerveza*, but hey, why waste
even a syllable? Just ask for a
birra instead. And remember
not to roll your Rs, **tico** style! If
you keep drinking **birras,** that
will probably take care of itself!

yodo

When coffee mixes with chlo-
rinated water, it approaches the
color of *iodine,* or **yodo.** Thus,
locals call *coffee* **yodo.** A headline read: "Tardes de lluvia con
un buen **yodo.**" "Rainy afternoons with a good *coffee.*"

churchill

Legend has it that some years ago in Puntarenas a San José doctor frequented a local ice cream parlor where a new treat had been invented: *a slushy with ice cream, cola syrup, and condensed milk.* The good doctor bore a striking resemblance to Winston Churchill, so whenever the employees saw him coming, they would say: "Here comes Churchill." To this day, this frosty treat is known as a **churchill.**

boli

Take any fruit juice, pour it into an oblong plastic bag, freeze it, and voilà! You have a **boli. Boli** was a brand name for this product years ago, but now it refers to *any local popsicle.*

pensando en los huevos del gallo

LITERAL MEANING:
thinking about the rooster's eggs

Last I checked, roosters don't lay eggs. This clever metaphor means *to daydream.* So if you lose yourself in thought, just announce: "Lo siento. **Estaba pensando en los huevos del gallo.**" "I'm sorry; *I was daydreaming.*"

R E L A T E D   T E R M S

gallo pinto

Gallo pinto means *spotted rooster,* but it is 100% chicken-less. It is rice and beans fried together with a touch of **cilantro**, or *coriander.* Add a fried egg and some ripe plantains, and that's a proper breakfast.

gallito

A **gallito** is not a little rooster, but rather a *small portion of food wrapped in a tortilla.* In reality, any small amount of food could be called a **gallito.** It is in essence the local term for *leftovers.*

andar pelada

LITERAL MEANING: to walk around peeled

If bananas were people, how would one feel if he had to walk in public peeled? Naked, right? For that reason, if a local walks around **pelada,** it means he or she is *lightly dressed.* When it's hot out, that sounds a-peeling, doesn't it?

Andar pelada also means *to be broke.*

barbudos

This literally means the *bearded ones*, but you won't find them in barbershops. Rather, it is a local dish: an *egg casserole with green beans.* So don't be uptight. Let your hair down and try some **barbudos!**

camanance

This word comes from Nahuatl terms for mouth and **nance,** a small yellow fruit native to Costa Rica. And the dimple was born. "¡Qué bonito el **camanance** de la güila!" "The girl's *dimple* is so cute!"

109

pulpería

Since **pulpo** means *octopus*, a foreigner could easily mistake a **pulpería** for some seafood outlet. In reality, though, this is the term for *small family-run convenience stores*. They sell everything from crackers to toilet paper and they are everywhere!

RELATED TERMS

110

natilla

Pronounced nah-TEE-yah. Here's an item you can pick up at the **pulpería**: *sour cream,* the perfect complement to your **gallo pinto.** In other Latin countries, it's known as **crema** or **crema ácida.**

111

soda

Sometimes a soda isn't a soda. If you fancy a carbonated beverage, ask for a **gaseosa.** But you might find that drink at a local **soda,** *a coffee shop or family-run restaurant.* I'll drink to that!

¡No se trague esa yuca!

LITERAL MEANING:
Don't swallow that cassava!

Yuca, or *cassava*, is a potato-like root that is quite tough and must be boiled at length to make it edible. Similarly hard to digest are other people's lies. For that reason, this culinary metaphor means: *Don't fall for those lies!*

————— **RELATED TERMS** —————

estar de chicha

Chicha is a fermented corn drink. If you put it in a bottle and cork it, watch out! The fermentation process will continue and the cork may pop. That's why **estar de chicha** means to *get very angry*.

jamar

This means *to eat*. "Vamos a **jamar** y luego salir a pasear." Translation: "Let's *eat* and then go out." Similarly, **jama** is *food*. A synonym is **monchar,** derived from the English *to munch*. Munchies anyone?

THE BRIGHT SIDE

como un ajito

LITERAL MEANING:
like a little garlic

Try this: peel a clove of garlic. Notice how shiny the surface is? This detail was not lost on the locals, who use garlic as a metaphor for extreme cleanliness. After giving your dog a bath, you might say: **Lo dejaron como un ajito.** In other words, *he's squeaky clean.* A man posted this classified: "Nissan 1200: **¡Hecho Un Ajito!**" "Nissan 1200: *Super clean!*"

RELATED TERMS

¡Qué limpiada!

As a child, you spend hours cleaning your room. How will your parents feel when they see it? Impressed! That's the idea behind this idiom that literally means, What a cleaning! It is like saying: *I am so impressed!*

chainear

Chainear was imported from the English verb *to shine.* For natives it means *to clean* or *make presentable.* "Dejemos el carro **chaineado** antes del viaje." "Let's give the car *a good cleaning* before we go."

buchaquita

A **buchaca** is a *bag* or *purse*. In some Latin countries, it is used to describe the pockets of a pool table. But for the natives here, it's where they keep their money: the piggy bank.

An article in *La Teja* commented: "Cuando nos sorprenden los imprevistos debemos pedir prestado para cubrirlos porque no tenemos una **buchaquita** capaz de salvarnos."

Translation: "When unexpected things come up, we have to borrow to cover them because we don't have a *piggy bank* capable of saving us."

Vieras que...

LITERAL MEANING:
You should see that...

If you really want to sound Costa Rican, start most of your sentences with this phrase. It translates to roughly: *You should have seen...* It's a formula not common in other Latin countries. **"¡Vieras que** un montón de gente estuvo en la playa!"
Translation: *"You should have seen it;* there were tons of people at the beach."

--- **RELATED TERMS** ---

¿Hay campo?

You are getting into a crowded bus and want to know if there is room for one more. So just ask: **¿Hay campo para uno más?** In other countries it would be more common to say: **¿Hay lugar?** or **¿Hay espacio?**

¡Tenga paz!

What all the terms on this page have in common is that they are unusual formulas to express ideas in Spanish. Here's one more: **¡Tenga paz!** It's the local way to say: *Calm down!* Peace be the journey.

¡Qué chiva!

LITERAL MEANING: What a female goat!

As we learned in term #56, locals call their girlfriends **cabras,** also female goats. And whatever we see through the eyes of love is beautiful. That's the meaning here. **"¡Qué chiva** su anillo!" "That's a *beautiful* ring!"

a cachete

LITERAL MEANING: to the cheek

Do you remember when you were a kid and the relatives would come over? For some unknown reason, they loved to squeeze our cheeks. It is as if they were some symbol of cuteness. **A cachete** follows this same principle. "¡La fiesta estuvo **a cachete!"** Translation: "The party was *great!*"

Voy p'al sobre.

LITERAL MEANING:
I am going to the envelope.

When we climb into bed at night and get under the covers, we are enveloped by them. That is the word picture here. **Voy pa'l sobre.**

Translation: *I'm going to hit the hay.*

———— **RELATED TERMS** ————

clavar el pico

This literally means to hammer your beak. Tropical birds like parrots usually bury their beaks into their feathers when they are ready to sleep. If someone says: **Voy a clavar el pico,** it means: *I'm going to take a nap.*

rulear

Yawn! Yet another verb for sleeping. "Mi abuela pasa **rule-ando** todas las tardes." Translation: "My grandmother spends all her afternoons *sleeping*."
"Todos **se rulean** en clase."
"Everyone *falls asleep* in class."

galleta

LITERAL MEANING: cracker

Bread has been around for centuries, but the cracker is a relative newcomer. At the time of its introduction in the country, it was considered to be superior to bread. For that reason, here it means to be *good* or *skilled* at something. "Ramón es una **galleta** para el estudio." Translation: "Ramón es *really good* at studying."

carga

LITERAL MEANING: load

A rich person might be described as loaded. In this local adjective, the person described is loaded with talent. "Pregúntele la respuesta. Ella es bien **carga** en las matemáticas." Translation: "Ask her the answer. She is *really smart* at math."

harina

LITERAL MEANING: flour

Need some dough—some cash? Well, in Costa Rica you don't have to add water. That because here *cash* isn't dough, it's **harina,** just plain flour. "¿Me presta un poco de **harina,** una teja aunque sea?"

Translation: "Can you loan me some *dough,* even if it's just 100 colones?"

papudo

LITERAL MEANING: potato-like

Ever seen a skinny potato? They are not common. In honor of the humble tuber, the adjective **papudo** alludes to what makes us fat in the wallet: wealth. A headline read: "Cristiano Ronaldo es el deportista más **papudo.**" Translation: "Cristiano Ronaldo is the *wealthiest* athlete." Fries anyone?

la última chupada del mango

LITERAL MEANING: the last suck on the mango

Ripe mangoes are especially sweet. In the end, all that remains is to suck on the pit and get out the last bit of goodness. So if someone considers himself that last chance at the mango, it means he thinks he is God's gift; *he's stuck up.*

bombeta

In Costa Rica there is a kind of bomb that doesn't explode, because a **bomba** is a *rhyming folkloric jingle,* often humorous and many times created on the spur of the moment. And the artist making it up is called a **bombeta.** Today the term refers to the person who wants to be *the center of attention, the class clown, the ham of the party.*

Si no hay perro, con gato se montea.

LITERAL MEANING: If there's no dog,
you can hunt with a cat.

No hound available for the deer hunt? No problem! Just
take the cat! That may not sound practical, but it's the
premise behind this comical saying. It essentially means:
Make do with what you have.

hacer un McGyver

Remember McGyver? In the late 1980s TV series he
was the secret government agent who always carried
a Swiss army knife and duct tape, which he used
ingeniously to get himself out of jams. His character has
been immortalized here with this verb, which means
to solve problems in unusual ways. Give the name a
Spanish pronunciation: *mahk-GEE-vuhr.* By the way,
have you seen the duct tape?

feria

Ever heard of *the baker's dozen?* The **feria** is essentially the same idea. The next time you go to the market and buy a dozen lemons or oranges, negotiate the price. Then, when they have been packed, say: **"Y ¿la feria?"**

Your excellent Costa Rican Spanish will bring a smile to the merchant's face, and he will throw in number 13 for free! Just with this tip, you will more than pay for the price of this book!

──────── **RELATED TERMS** ────────

pulsear

Ever arm wrestle anyone? In Spanish *arm wrestling* is **echar un pulso.** So **pulsear** means *to convince, to be persistent.* **"Pulséele** a su abuelo para que le regale dinero."
"Pester your grandpa until he gives you money."

zarpe

Zarpar is the Spanish verb for *setting sail.* But when you are down at the local bar and are ready to head home, just tell the bartender: **¡Zarpe!** In this context, it means: *"I'll have a nightcap!"* Just try not to make any waves.

69

pura vida

University of Costa Rica researcher Victor Sánchez reports that this quintessential local phrase has its origins in a 1955 Mexican movie entitled *Pura Vida*. In it the actor Clavillazo uses the phrase **pura vida** 13 times. So if someone asks how you are, just say: **¡Pura vida!** That means you are doing *great*. What was that 1955 movie like? **¡Pura vida!** It was *fabulous!* And it is alive and well today as the national buzzword.

--- **RELATED TERMS** ---

¡Qué dicha!

This exclamation means: *What a blessing!* or *How fortunate!*
"¡Qué dicha que trajo su sombrilla! Está cayendo un baldazo."
"How fortunate that you brought your umbrella! It is really pouring down."

¡Qué guaba!

Guaba is a long green fruit filled with sweet white seeds. But locals equate it with a stroke of luck.
"¿Vio ese gol que metió? **¡Qué guaba!"**
"Did you see that goal he made? That was *a lucky shot!*"

70

tuanis

Some say **tuanis** comes from the English expression *too nice.* Others claim it is Malespín code for **bueno.** (See **brete,** term #71.) Whatever its origins, **tuanis** is a frequent utterance throughout the country. An events company posted this: "Hacemos de tus eventos algo **tuanis.**" "We make your events something *special.*"

"¡Qué **tuanis** la fiesta!" "What a *great* party!"

--- RELATED TERMS ---

buena nota

Nothing make parents happier than when their children get good grades. This phrase liter- ally means *good grade.*
"Vieras que Jaime es **buena nota.**"
"That Jaime is a *really nice guy.*"

la tapa del perol

This literally means *the lid of a pot.* The lid obviously sits on top; for that reason, here it means *the top, the best.* "En el fútbol los brasileños son **la tapa del perol.**"
"In soccer the Brazilians are the *cream of the crop.*"

Páseme el serrucho a ver si me hago cosquillas.

LITERAL MEANING:
Pass me the saw to see if I can tickle myself.

Has anyone ever told you a joke that wasn't funny? How did you respond? Maybe you asked: 'Was I supposed to laugh?' In Costa Rica, just say this.

———— **RELATED TERMS** ————

¡Qué vacilón!

Here's another phrase you will here countless times in the country. If you hear something comical, just say this. It means: *How funny!* or *How hilarious!* "La fiesta fue un **vacilón.**" "The party was *a lot of fun.*"

Me agarró la payasa.

This literally means, *The lady clown grabbed me.* And clowns make us laugh, sometimes so hard that it is difficult to stop. When that happens and you can't ditch the giggles, just say this line. It's like saying: *I lost it.*

ins*derspanish

Costa Rican Spanish

6

THE DARK SIDE

sopa de techo

LITERAL MEANING:
roof soup

People say that soup is good food, but that's not the case here. Ever had a night in which you couldn't sleep? What do you look at? If you stay in bed and open your eyes, you will be gazing at the ceiling, or the roof. If so, then you are figuratively eating roof soup, or **sopa de techo!** Yawn!

---------------- **RELATED TERMS** ----------------

bostezo

This literally means a *yawn*. It's the local term for a *boring person*. "No quiero salir con él, es un **bostezo**." "I don't want to go out with him. He's such a *bore.*" When referring to such a stick in the mud, you just exclaim: **¡Qué bostezo!** *What a bore!*

¡Qué pereza!

Remember what it was like to sit in the class of a boring teacher? Did you feel motivated? Likely not. It only made you feel lazier. This saying literally means: *What laziness!* But the real meaning is: *How boring!*

74

Se armó la gorda.

LITERAL MEANING: The fat lady has armed herself.

In 1968 in Spain a revolt that was rising up against Queen Isabel II was nicknamed **La Gorda,** or the fat lady. Since then, when people say, **se armó la gorda,** they mean that *a conflict is imminent.* "Allí viene la policía. Ahorá sí **se armó la gorda."** Translation: "There come the police. *All hell is going to break loose."*

vina

In San José's Barrio México there once lived a certain Etelvina de Avendaño, who became a notorious gossip. Based on her experience, a popular comedic radio program was created titled *Viniando con doña Vina*, which roughly translates to *Butting in with Ms. Busybody.* To this day a **vina** is a *busybody* or *buttinsky.* "Cuidado con esa **doña Vina.** Se mete en todo." "Watch out for that *busybody.* She sticks her nose in everything."

caerle todo el mundo

LITERAL MEANING:
to have everyone fall on you

A united front is hard to beat. This phrase speaks to those times when everyone is against you. "Cuando sugerí cancelar la vacación, **me cayó todo el mundo.**" Translation: "When I suggested cancelling vacation, *everyone ganged up on me.*"

———— **RELATED TERMS** ————

carbonear

Where there's no wood, the fire goes out. But throw coal in, a source of carbon, and the fire grows more. "Mi ex novia **carboneó** a mi novia actual para que me dejara." "My ex-girlfriend *egged on* my current girlfriend to leave me."

comerse la bronca

A **bronca** is a *conflict* or *problem*. So if you figuratively eat it, it means you are taking the blame. "Cuando su equipo perdió, el portero **se comió la bronca.**" "When his team lost, the goalie *took the blame.*" Eat crow and grow!

¡Qué camote!

LITERAL MEANING:
What a sweet potato!

Local writer Dennis Meléndez suggests that in a psychiatric hospital just outside of San José doctors experimented with patients by having them participate in the cultivation of sweet potatoes. Hence, sweet potatos became synonymous with having a screw loose. So the next time you hear a crazy idea, just say: **¡Qué camote!**

--- RELATED TERMS ---

bicho raro

A **bicho raro** is a *strange insect.* We might feel like that poor bug when we are the new ones. "Como no conocí a nadie en la fiesta, me sentí como un **bicho raro.**" "Since I didn't know anyone at the party, I felt *out of place.*"

Le patina el coco.

This literally means: *His coconut is slipping.* Costa Ricans humorously refer to their heads as coconuts. So if your "coconut" is slipping, it means the lights are on, but nobody's home, and the elevator doesn't go to the top floor. Coconut anyone?

Se me para la peluca.

LITERAL MEANING: My wig is standing on end.

In English when our hair stands on end, we are frightened. But for locals the hyperbole is even greater: their entire symbolic wig stands up. "Cuando escuché del accidente de mi abuela, **se me paró la peluca.**" "When I heard about my grandma's accident, *my hair stood on end.*"

en alas de cucaracha

LITERAL MEANING: on a cockroach's wings

Ready to ride the wings of a cockroach? I didn't think so. We generally try to get as far away from cockroaches as possible. And we do the same with danger. "Cuando comenzaron los despidos en la empresa, todos quedaron **en alas de cucaracha.**" Translation: "When layoffs began at the company, all the workers were *waiting for the other shoe to drop.*"

acabangado

There are days when we are ready to climb the highest mountain, and then there are others in which we can't even climb out of bed. For these latter moments, we have this word, which means *depressed*.
"Desde que perdió su empleo, Raúl anda todo **acabangado**."

Translation: "Every since Raúl lost his job, he has been walking around *all depressed*."

RELATED TERMS

achantado

In local lingo, **chante** means *laziness*. If someone is said to be **achantado,** he is *lazy*. "Enrique es tan **achantado** que nadie lo quiere contratar." "Enrique is so *lazy* that no one wants to hire him." Conversely, **Achánteme** means: *Wait for me.*

dolor de jupa

If you are feeling a little depressed and lazy, it may be that you have a **dolor de jupa**—the local term for a *headache*. **Jupa** means *head*, but if you are described as **jupón,** you are *stubborn*. So stay humble and don't get a big **jupa.**

Está pa'l tigre.

LITERAL MEANING:
It's for the tiger.

Years ago at the Bolívar Parque Zoo in San José, old, sickly animals met a grisly fate: they were fed to the tigers. As a result, this phrase came into vogue to mean *worthless, washed up.* "Ese televisor ya no sirve; **está p'al tigre."** Translation: "That television no longer works. *It's ready for the trash heap.*"

RELATED TERMS
---

jumarse

An activity that will make you prematurely ready for the tiger (see the term above) is this verb, which means *to get drunk.*
"Federico **se juma** todos los sábados."
"Federico *gets wasted* every Saturday."

tapis

Drunks are called **tapis,** a term derived from **tapa**—the beer bottle cap. "Esa calle está llena de **tapis."** "That street is filled with *drunks.*" The inebriated are also **bolos,** literally *bowling pins.* That's because they are always falling down.

cerrado como bombillo

LITERAL MEANING:
closed like a light bulb

Your light bulb has burned out. Would you attempt to open it and change the filament? Impossible! It is completely sealed and can't be fixed. And so are the close-minded. "Rodolfo nunca quiere probar cosas nuevas. Es **cerrado como bombillo**." Translation: "Rodolfo never wants to try new things. He is *close-minded*."

———— R E L A T E D   T E R M S ————

baboso

In Spanish, *saliva* is called **baba**. Since those who are no longer in their right minds may unwittingly drool, **baboso** has come to mean *foolish*, or *stupid*. "No sea **baboso**. Así no se hace." "Don't be *foolish*. That's not the way you do it."

mozote

Ticos make a drink, or **fresco,** from a plant called **mozote.** The plant's juices tend to be somewhat viscous, which fact reminded locals of **baba** (See term #167.) **Mozote** came to mean *simple-minded*. "Seas **mozote."** "Don't be *silly."*

81

chapulín

LITERAL MEANING:
grasshopper

Today's criminals use their weapons to steal at will. But the simple thief may do no more than hop a fence. That led to *young bandits* being dubbed **chapulines,** literally *grasshoppers.* "Ayer el policía agarró a cuatro **chapulines** en mi barrio." Translation: "Yesterday the police caught four *young burglars* in my neighborhood."

---------- **RELATED TERMS** ----------

bote

Botar la basura means *to throw out the trash.* From this verb we likely have received **bote,** where the figurative trash of the justice system ends up: *jail.* "Los chapulines terminaron en el **bote.**" "The thieves ended up in *jail.*"

cara 'e barro

Playing cards? Then put on your best poker face. But what about a *clay* face? That's what this local expression literally means. Here it means a *scoundrel,* a *fake.* "Ese **cara 'e barro** me engañó." "That *dirty scoundrel* duped me."

arroz con mango

LITERAL MEANING:
rice with mango

Hungry for some chicken and rice? Delicious! But what about rice and mango? Disgusting! It's a combination that doesn't work. Logically, then, **arroz con mango** means *confusion* or *chaos*. "Cuando chocaron los dos trailers, se formó un tremendo **arroz con mango.**" "When the two semis collided, all *chaos* broke out."

———— R E L A T E D   T E R M S ————

embarcarse

Want to work on a ship? Most don't. Who wants to leave the family for weeks on end? But if problems arise, you might not have a choice. "No **se embarque** comprando ese yate." "Don't *get yourself into trouble* buying that yacht."

hacer la masaguada

Want a good grade? You might have to butter up your teacher. But here you'll have to water her dough. "Sandra le **hacía la masaguada** a su patrono para ver si la ascendía." "Sandra was *kissing* her employer's *butt* in hopes of a promotion."

Tengo un perro amarrado.

LITERAL MEANING:
I have a dog tied up.

Dogs bark. When we are in debt, our creditors may also bark—pestering us until we pay. So this phrase means: *I have a debt.* Similarly, he who *borrows money but never pays it back* is an **amarraperros**. When you finally *pay your debt*, it can be said that you let your dog go (**soltar el perro**). Just don't bark up the wrong tree!

───── **RELATED TERMS** ─────

agarrado

Agarrar means *to grab* or *to hold on to.* In this case, if a person is **agarrado,** he is clutching his money.
"No le pida nada a don Manuel; es **agarrado.**"
"Don't ask don Manuel for anything; he's *stingy.*"

dar por la nuca

As a foreigner, you not only have to watch your back, but your neck as well! This idiom, literally *to hit on the neck*, means *to charge an exorbitant price.*
"¡Diay! ¿Por qué me quiere **dar por la nuca?"** "Hey, why are you trying *to gouge me?*"

polo

Society today is divided into classes, and the **polo** drew the short straw. It means *low class*.

"No compre esa blusa, es tan **pola**."
Translation: "Don't buy that blouse; it's such *cheap quality*."

"No sea **polo**."
Translation: "Don't be *crude*."

---------- RELATED TERMS ----------

pachuco

Pachuco is a derogatory term for uneducated and often unemployed youths known for their vulgar speech and dubious behavior. "No se meta con él; es un **pachuco**." "Don't get involved with him; he's *bad news*."

gajo

A **gajo** is a slice of lemon. But when your purchase turns out to be a lemon, it means *of poor quality*, or *shoddy*. "Desde que se compró ese **gajo** de carro, ¿cuánto ha ahorrado?" "Since you bought that *cheap* car, how much have you saved?"

mala nota

LITERAL MEANING:
bad grade

Ever get a bad grade in school? If so, surely you didn't run home to tell your parents; it's shameful. Similarly, when a person is locally called **mala nota,** it means that they have been graded as *unkind* or *inept*. "Esa mesera es **mala nota;** ni caso me hace." Translation: "That waitress is *terrible*. She doesn't even notice me."

---- **RELATED TERMS** ----

pinche

Considered a vulgarity in Mexico, **pinche** is totally innocent here. It alludes to the one who is pinching his pennies to such an extreme that he has become tightfisted. "No seas tan **pinche.**" "Don't be so *stingy.*"

espeso

When we marry, we promise to do so during thick and thin. This word is for those *thick* times. "Las cosas se están poniendo **espesas** entre Daniel y Laura." "Things are getting *pretty bad* between Daniel and Laura." The plot thickens!

Estamos limpios.

LITERAL MEANING: We are clean.

In English we equate poverty with filth: *dirt* poor. But **ticos** see it from another perspective. When there is no money, they are "clean." "Mi empresa cerró hace un año y ahora **estamos limpios.**"

Translation: "My company closed up a year ago, and now we are *dirt poor.*"

--- RELATED TERMS ---

joder

Here's another verb that is a vulgarity elsewhere. In Costa Rica it just means *to bother*, or *to be ruined*. "Deje de **joderme.**"
"Stop *bothering* me."
In other another context:
"Se jodió el televisor."
"The television *broke.*"

presa

This literally means a *dam*. But when traffic is at a standstill, it is as if the collective fleet forms a dam. For that reason, here it is a *traffic jam*. "No salgas a las cinco. Es pura *presa.*" "Don't go out at five o'clock. It's nothing but a *traffic jam.*"

87

miar fuera del tarro

LITERAL MEANING:
to urinate outside the can

In our zeal to show how smart we are, we may answer questions on topics that we know nothing about, and we end up peeing outside the can, so to speak. (See also **La sacó del estadio,** term #19.) This is similar to *being in left field.* Moral of the story? Think outside the box, but pee *inside* the can.

───── **RELATED TERMS** ─────

detrás del palo

Maybe the reason you are urinating outside the can (see above) is that you are behind the proverbial tree. This idiom means the same. "Mae, está **detrás del palo.** Mejor cierre el pico." "Dude, you're *off your rocker.* Zip it."

pifia

A **pifia** is a *mistake.* One site reported: "El gobierno tuvo que corregir la **pifia** de 80 metros en el diseño de la carretera." "The government had to correct an 80-meter *blunder* in the design of the highway."

¡Manda la parada!

Ever invite someone to come to a party or to do something for you, only to have them say no and offer a flimsy excuse? If so, this is the perfect **tico** comeback.

"Usted es mi mejor amigo y ¿no va a venir a mi fiesta? **¡Manda la parada!"**

Translation: "You're my best friend and you're not coming to my party? *Give me a break!*"

--- RELATED TERMS ---

¡Qué cáscara!

This literally means: *What a shell!* and suggests an ulterior motive. **"¡Qué cáscara!** ¿No ven que el defensa ni lo tocó? Puro teatro." *"What nerve!* Don't they see that the defense didn't touch him. What an act!"

enjachar

If looks could kill, the planet would be nearly empty. **Enjachar** means *to stare down.* "Después de clavar el baloncesto, LeBron **enjachó** a su oponente." "After the dunk, LeBron *stared down* his opponent."

¡Tome pa'l pinto!

This is classic trash talk, Costa Rican style, and literally means: *Take this for the gallo pinto*. Imagine the scene: You are in a tight soccer game. Finally, you break through the defense and score the game-winning goal! To top things off, you say, **¡Tome pa'l pinto!** to the goalie. It's like boasting in English: *"Look who's laughing now!"* Or perhaps: *"How do you like them apples?"* Or even: *"Stick that in your pipe and smoke it."*

RELATED TERMS

¡Tome chichi!

Here's more trash talk in this headline: **"¡Tome chichi!** Modelo plus size le manda tremendo ubicatex a tuitero que quiso humillarla."** *"Take that!* Plus size model puts tweeter who tried to humiliate her in his place."* Yikes!

sacarse el clavo

This literally means *to take the nail out*. When we are wronged, a symbolic nail is put in us. When we take it out, we get even. "Paulo Vargas **se sacó el clavo** y se puso la chema de líder." "Paulo Vargas *got even* and put on the leader's shirt."

Sias tan mi amor.

LITERAL MEANING: Be so much my love.

At times, pity moves us to view fools with certain affection. When a baby does something silly, we might say: Bless his little heart! "Nuestro abuelito de repente bajó su pantalón y orinó en medio del parque. **Sias tan mi amor.**" "Our grandpa suddenly dropped his pants and urinated in the middle of the park. *Bless his heart.*" In other contexts it could mean: *Don't be so ungrateful!* or *Don't be so cruel!*

rayar

Rayar literally means *to scratch.* But in this case, it means *to pass on the highway.*
"Rogelio se tiró a **rayar** en pista y llegó una hora antes."
"Rogelio was *passing* the cars on the highway and got there an hour early."

91

Que no le den por la jupa.

LITERAL MEANING:
Don't let them hit you upside the head.

Of all our body parts, the head is of vital importance. Without our mental faculties intact, it would be impossible to make wise decisions. That is especially true when we go shopping. This phrase, then, means: *Don't get scammed.* Just a little heads up!

———— **RELATED TERMS** ————

Me sacaron el sirope.

Blood is thicker than water. Even so, it may not literally have the consistency of syrup, as suggested in this hyperbolic speech, which means: *They knocked the snot out of me.* Sorry, Aunt Jemima.

cachar

Cachar is a loan from the English *to catch*—only in this instance it refers to an illicit catch: *stealing.* "¡Diay! ¿Quién **cachó** mis cachos?" "Hey, who *swiped* my shoes?" We hope this activity will never catch on with the majority.

THE GOLDEN FERIA

The Golden
FERIA

Usted es más tico que el gallo pinto.

LITERAL MEANING: You are more Costa Rican than gallo pinto.

Gallo pinto is a staple of the local cuisine. So if you are more Costa Rican that that, we tip our hat to you. If a local tells you this, you have indeed mastered the local Spanish—there is no greater compliment!

As the proud owner of more than 200 key Costa Rican words, phrases, and sayings, we urge you: keep listening. When you hear a new word or phrase, write it down. Find out what it means. You will be well on your way to speaking Spanish like a native, one country at a time! So put that **jupa** to work! We trust that your newfound proficiency will truly be **pura vida.**

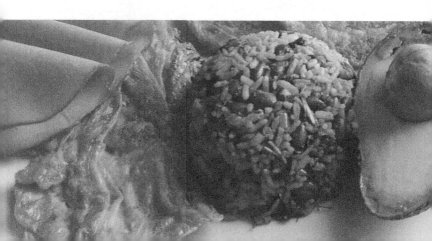

ACKNOWLEDGMENTS

IN 1996 my wife and I first visited Costa Rica, at the behest of our friend Xinia de Jaén. On that initial trip Xinia was missing some ingredients for a meal, but with determination, she pressed forward, uttering this local saying: **Cuando no hay perro, con gato se montea.** (See term #133.)

Though eager to venture into the local Spanish, I at first confused **montearse**, *to hunt*, with **montarse**, *to ride*. So later I told her: **Cuando no hay perro, hasta se puede montar un gato.** That literally means: When there's no dog, you can always ride a cat!

My botched attempt at Costa Rican Spanish left Xinia in stitches, but it was the humble beginning of learning yet another local Spanish. The friendship made with Xinia's family has persisted over the years and they have been instrumental in the creation of this new volume of country-specific Spanish.

Additionally, I thank my wife Moraima for her continued encouragement and suggestions. Thanks as well to Jason and Emily Provchy for the office space provided during the preparation of this volume.

Much gratitude goes also to Diego and Tatiana Chavarría, Esteban and Gloriana Jaén, as well as Andrés and Natividad González—all native speakers—for clearing up details about some of Costa Rica's traditional sayings.

And, lastly, I am indebted to the people of Costa Rica for their painstaking patience with all of us foreigners who have learned your most lyrical version of Spanish one explanation at a time.

insi der*spanish*

Costa Rican Spanish

INDEX

E

F

G

H

J

L

PHOTO CREDITS

COSTA RICAN
SPANISH
SPEAK LIKE A NATIVE!

LEE JAMISON

insider spanish

GUATEMALAN
SPANISH
SPEAK LIKE A NATIVE!

LEE JAMISON

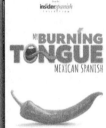

insider spanish

my **BURNING**
TONGUE
MEXICAN SPANISH

LEE JAMISON

Become an
ins**i**der
What are you waiting for?

insider

NICARAGUAN
SPANISH
SPEAK LIKE A NATIVE!

LEE JAMISON

insider spanish

PANAMANIAN
SPANISH
SPEAK LIKE A NATIVE!

LEE JAMISON

Made in the USA
Monee, IL
21 April 2023